Beginners
Complete
SLOW
COOKER

Ellen Hope

Beginners Complete Slow Cooker

ISBN: 9798428530568

Copyright © 2022 Ellen Hope

CONTENTS

Slow Cooking 101

Do you love the smell of a home-cooked meal, but don't have enough time to cook during the week? If so, a slow cooker may be the perfect appliance for you! A slow cooker is a device that cooks food slowly over a long period of time. This makes it perfect for busy people who want to come home to a warm, cooked meal.

What is a Slow Cooker?

Slow cookers have been around for over 40 years and are one of the most popular kitchen appliances. A slow cooker is a cost-effective, easy, time-saving, and healthy way to cook food. The slow cooker is great for cooking soups, stews, chili, and roasts. It is also a great way to cook tough cuts of meat so they are tender and moist. Slow cooking allows food to simmer slowly which results in a more nutritious and delicious meal.

A slow cooker is a great way to cook food without having to watch it constantly. The food cooks slowly and evenly, so it doesn't burn or stick. You can use a slow cooker to cook almost anything, from soup to roast chicken.

The three most common types of slow cookers are programmable, manual, and automatic. Programmable slow cookers have a timer that allows you to set the cooking time and temperature. When the food has finished cooking they switch to a 'keep warm' setting to avoid overcooking. Manual slow cookers do not have a timer, so you need to be present when the food is being cooked. Automatic slow cookers turn off after a certain amount of time has passed.

There are three common settings for a slow cooker: low, high, and warm. Low is typically 200 degrees Fahrenheit, while high is 300 degrees Fahrenheit. The warm setting is used to keep food warm after it has been cooked.

Slow Cooker Sizes & Shapes

Slow cookers come in different shapes and sizes, so it is important to choose one that will fit your needs. Some recipes may call for a large or small slow cooker. When choosing a size, you should consider how many people you will be cooking for. A four-quart slow cooker is a good size for one or two people, while an eight-quart slow cooker is good for four to six people.

It is difficult to get the balance right and you ultimately should choose based on what you intend to use it for most. If you want to cook large pot roasts you will need a 6-8 quart slow cooker but this will likely be too large for everyday use and can lead to dried-out meat if you're just cooking a simple stew.

The shape of your slow cooker will also affect what you can cook in it. The benefits of an oval slow cooker over a round one are that the oval slow cooker can fit more food inside and is better for larger cuts of meat.

The main benefits of a round slow cooker over an oval slow cooker are that they are easier to store and they cook food more evenly. Round slow cookers take up less space in your kitchen cabinets, and the food is cooked more evenly because the heat is spread more evenly throughout the pot.

COOKING TIMES

The cooking time will depend on the recipe you are using and your particular model of slow cooker. It is important to read the recipe carefully before you begin cooking. Pasta, fish, or chicken dishes will require much less cooking time than tougher beef or pork cuts. If a recipe says 6-8 hours then it should be ready to eat after 6 hours but you should check any meat is cooked through before serving.

Pasta can be added to the slow cooker around 30-45 minutes before the end of cooking.

Fish requires only 1-2 hours on high or 2-3 hours on the low setting.

Chicken requires 3-4 hours on high and 4-6 hours on low. A whole chicken will need 5-6 hours on high and 8-10 hours on low.

Beef, pork, or lamb generally require around 3-4 hours on low and 6-8 hours on high but largr joints will need 6-7 hours on high and 8-10 hours on low.

Different makes and models of slow cookers will cook at slightly different temperatures, so spend some time experimenting and getting to know your slow cooker. If your food isn't cooked by the end of the cooking time, try increasing the temperature. If your food is dried out then reduce the heat or cooking time.

You can speed up the cooking time of larger cuts but chopping the meat into smaller pieces. You can also avoid meat drying out by waiting to cut it after cooking - putting chicken breasts in whole, for instance, rather than cubing them first.

SLOW COOKING BENEFITS

There are many benefits of using a slow cooker. A slow cooker is an inexpensive and convenient way to cook food. It is a good option for low budgeters as it can be used just about anywhere and on any day of the week.

- They are cost-effective because you can buy cheaper cuts of meat and they will still be tender after cooking in the slow cooker.

They are very easy to use; you just add the ingredients and turn them on.

They take up very little space so they're an ideal gadget for smaller kitchens.

Slow cookers also free up time because you don't have to watch them constantly as you would with a stovetop pot.

Slow cookers are healthy and nutritious because they don't produce a lot of fat or grease as some other cooking methods do. They also lock in the nutrients that would otherwise be lost with other cooking methods.

Tips & Tricks

slow cooker is a great way to cook food without having to watch it constantly. The food ooks slowly and evenly, so it doesn't burn or stick. You can use a slow cooker to cook almost nything, from soup to roast chicken. In this article, we'll show you how to use a slow cooker, nd we'll give you some recipes to get started.

Don't overfill your slow cooker. This will prevent the food from cooking evenly.

Don't put the slow cooker on high heat if you're going to be gone all day. The food will cook too quickly and might be overcooked or burnt by the time you get back.

Many recipes can be converted to slow cooker meals by reducing the amount of liquid used. For example, if a recipe calls for one cup of broth, only use half a cup in the slow cooker. This will help prevent the food from becoming too watery. Barely any liquid is lost when cooking in a slow cooker so you don't need to add as much liquid as you would when cooking on a higher heat setting. Ingredients like meat and mushrooms will release a lot of their own juices too, so you should take this into account when converting recipes.

Some people believe that all meat should be browned before it's added to the slow cooker to seal in flavor and add another taste dimension. Others believe you shouldn't do this as you prevent the juices from escaping into the cooking liquid as well as possibly drying out the meat and adding unnecessary cooking time. Neither approach is right or wrong, which option you choose is up to your own personal preference. In this book we've included browning but feel free to skip this step if you want to.

Finally, don't forget to add any herbs or spices at the beginning of the cooking process so that they can infuse the dish with flavor.

conclusion, slow cookers are a great way to make delicious, home-cooked meals without aving to spend all day in the kitchen. The recipes in this book will show you how to make the ost of your slow cooker, so you can come home to a warm and hearty meal after a long day.

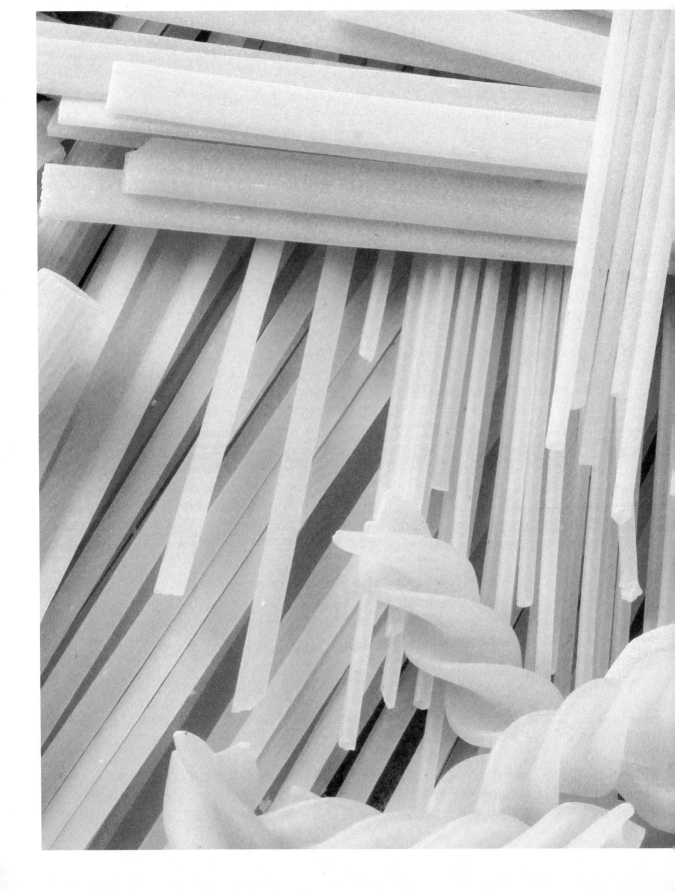

PASTA

You can cook pasta in the slow cooker by adding it directly in the sauce that you plan to serve it with. Pasta doesn't require much cooking time in a slow cooker and can be added to the pot around the last hour of cooking. If you're using a slow cooker to make a sauce or soup, add the pasta during the last 30 to 45 minutes of cooking time.

Check the pasta for doneness about 10 minutes before the cooking time is up to make sure it doesn't overcook. If the pasta is cooked through, turn off the slow cooker and allow it to sit for about 5 minutes to absorb the sauce.

SPAGHETTI & MEATBALLS

Spaghetti and meatballs is a classic dish that can be made in so many ways. But, what makes this slow cooker version so good? The answer is simple: the sauce. A slow cooker can bring out all the flavors of the sauce ingredients, resulting in a delicious and hearty meal. The meat cooks perfectly without drying out and the flavors are amazing!

INGREDIENTS

FOR THE MEATBALLS:

1 LB GROUND BEEF

1/2 CUP BREAD CRUMBS

1/2 CUP PARMESAN, GRATED

1 EGG

1/4 TSP GARLIC POWDER

1/4 TSP SALT

1/4 TSP BLACK PEPPER

6 OZ SPAGHETTI

4 OZ PARMESAN CHEESE,

FOR THE SAUCE:

1/2 LB PANCETTA, DICED

1 ONION

2 CANS CHOPPED TOMATOES

1/2 TEASPOON DRIED BASIL

1/2 TEASPOON DRIED OREGANO

1/4 TEASPOON BLACK PEPPER

3 CLOVES GARLIC, MINCED

8 OZ MASCARPONE CHEESE

Serves 6-8

METHOD

1. In a large skillet over medium heat, cook the pancetta until crisp.

2. Drain on paper towels and remove any excess fat. Add the onion and cook until translucent, about 5 minutes.

3. Stir in the tomatoes, basil, oregano, pepper, and garlic. Bring to a simmer and cook for 10 minutes. stir through the mascarpone until melted and add to the slow cooker.

4. In a large bowl, combine ground beef, bread crumbs, Parmesan cheese, egg, garlic powder, salt, and pepper. Mix well. Shape into 24 meatballs. Sear the meatballs if desired and place meatballs in the slow cooker.

5. In a small bowl, combine spaghetti sauce and water. Pour over meatballs. cover and cook on low for 6-8 hours or until meatballs are cooked through.

6. Serve over cooked spaghetti and sprinkle with parmesan cheese.

TIP This recipe makes a large batch that's perfect for freezing. To save time you can use a jar of bolognese sauce instead of making your own.

LAZY MACARONI & CHEESE

Macaroni and cheese is one of those nostalgic dishes that we all love because we first experienced it when were little kids. It's one of those dishes that we continue making and enjoying as adults. If you're looking for a quick slow cooker meal then you can't beat macaroni and cheese for speed. It's ready to eat in about an hour!

INGREDIENTS

1 LB ELBOW MACARONI

2 CUPS CHEDDAR CHEESE, SHREDDED

1/2 CUP GRUYERE CHEESE, SHREDDED

3 TBSP ALL-PURPOSE FLOUR

1 TSP SALT

1/4 TSP BLACK PEPPER

2 CUPS WHOLE MILK

1/4 CUP UNSALTED BUTTER

PARMESAN CHEESE OR BREADCRUMBS TO SERVE (OPTIONAL)

METHOD

1. In a saucepan, heat the milk and butter over medium heat until the butter has melted.

2. Slowly add the flour making stirring continuously until it is all combined.

3. Add the Gruyere and 1 1/2 cups of cheddar along with salt, and pepper and stir until the cheese has melted.

4. Pour the cheese sauce into the slow cooker and add the pasta. Stir well to combine and cover the mixture with the remaining cheddar.

5. Cover and cook for around 30-45 minutes or until pasta is softened.

6. If desired transfer to a grill safe pan and sprinkle with parmesan cheese or breadcrumbs. Toast under the grill for a few minutes to crisp up before serving.

Serves 4

SLOW BAKED ZITI

Baked Ziti is a dish made of ziti pasta and a meat sauce. The dish can also include cheese and vegetables. Baked Ziti is typically oven-baked, but can also be cooked in a slow cooker. This easy slow cooker Baked Ziti recipe is perfect for a busy weeknight!

INGREDIENTS

1 LB LEAN GROUND BEEF

1/2 TSP GARLIC POWDER

1/2 TSP ONION POWDER

1/2 TSP ITALIAN SEASONING

1/4 TSP SALT

1/4 TSP BLACK PEPPER

1 JAR (24 OZ) MARINARA SAUCE

1 CAN (15 OZ) DICED TOMATOES

3 TBSP CHOPPED FRESH PARSLEY

2 TBSP CHOPPED FRESH BASIL

8 OZ ZITI PASTA

6 OZ SHREDDED MOZZARELLA CHEESE

1/2 CUP GRATED PARMESAN CHEESE

METHOD

1. In a large bowl, combine ground beef, garlic powder, onion powder, Italian seasoning, salt, and black pepper. Mix well.

2. In a slow cooker, spread marinara sauce over the bottom. Place beef mixture in the cooker and spread evenly.

3. Top with diced tomatoes, parsley, and basil.

4. Cover and cook on low for 6 to 7 hours or on high for 3 to 4 hours.

5. 30 Minutes before the end of the cooking time, stir in the ziti pasta.

6. Fifteen minutes before the end of cooking time, stir in mozzarella cheese and Parmesan cheese until well blended.

7. Cover and continue cooking until pasta is cooked and cheese is melted and bubbly.

Serves 4

RAVIOLI WITH TOMATO SAUCE

This recipe for slow cooker Ravioli with Meat Sauce is an easy and convenient way to make a hearty and filling meal. The ingredients are staples that you may already have in your pantry, and the end result is a dish that is sure to please.

INGREDIENTS

1 LB GROUND BEEF

1 (25 OZ) JAR OF YOUR FAVORITE PASTA SAUCE

1 (15 OZ) CAN OF DICED TOMATOES

1/2 TSP GARLIC POWDER

1/2 TSP ITALIAN SEASONING

1/4 TSP SALT

1/4 TSP BLACK PEPPER

16 OZ CHEESE RAVIOLI

1/2 CUP GRATED PARMESAN CHEESE

METHOD

1. In a large bowl, combine pasta sauce, diced tomatoes, ground beef, garlic powder, Italian seasoning, salt, pepper.

2. Mix well and spread the mixture in the bottom of a slow cooker.

3. Cover and cook on low heat for 6-8 hours or on high heat for 4-6 hours.

4. Around 45 minutes before the end of the cooking time add cheese ravioli.

Sprinkle with Parmesan cheese to serve.

Serves 4-6

SLOW COOKER LASAGNE

Slow cookers are a great way to make a delicious lasagna with little effort. The ingredients are simply layered in the slow cooker, and the lasagna cooks slowly all day long. This is a perfect dish to make on a busy day when you don't have time to cook a meal from scratch.

INGREDIENTS

1 LB GROUND BEEF

1/2 CUP CHOPPED ONION

1 GARLIC CLOVE, MINCED

1 (15 OZ**)** CAN TOMATO SAUCE

1 (6 OZ**)** CAN TOMATO PASTE

1 TSP SUGAR

1/2 TSP ITALIAN SEASONING

1/4 TSP SALT

1/4 TSP BLACK PEPPER

9 LASAGNA PASTA SHEETS

15 OZ RICOTTA CHEESE

1 EGG

2 CUPS MOZZARELLA CHEESE, GRATED

METHOD

1. In a large skillet, cook ground beef, onion, and garlic over medium heat until meat is browned; drain. Stir in tomato sauce, tomato paste, sugar, Italian seasoning, salt, and pepper.

2. Spread 1/3 of the beef mixture in the bottom of a lightly greased 3-quart slow cooker. Arrange 3 pasta sheets over the beef mixture. Combine ricotta cheese and egg; spread over pasta. Sprinkle with 1 cup mozzarella cheese. Repeat layers of beef mixture, pasta, ricotta mixture, and mozzarella cheese two times.

3. Cover and cook on low for 4-5 hours or until pasta is tender.

Serves 4

BEEF

Slow cooker beef recipes are a great way to cook a tough cut of meat until it's fall-apart tender. The long, slow cooking process breaks down the connective tissues in the beef, resulting in a moist and juicy final dish.

The three most popular cuts of beef to cook in the slow cooker are chuck roast, brisket, and short ribs.

No matter the recipe you follow, slow cooked beef is always a hearty and filling dish that can warm you up on a cold winters day.

BEEF & BROCCOLI

Beef and broccoli is a classic dish that is often made in a wok with a sticky sauce. This version is made in a slow cooker with a simple sauce. The beef is cooked until it is tender and the broccoli is cooked until it is crisp-tender.

INGREDIENTS

LB FLANK STEAK, TRIMMED AND SLICED INTO THIN STRIPS

1/2 TSP GARLIC POWDER

1/4 TSP ONION POWDER

1/4 TSP GROUND GINGER

1/4 TSP BLACK PEPPER

TBSP SOY SAUCE

TBSP HONEY

TBSP VEGETABLE OIL, DIVIDED

LARGE HEAD BROCCOLI, CUT INTO FLORETS

CLOVES GARLIC, MINCED

SESAME SEEDS TO SERVE (OPTIONAL)

METHOD

1. In a large bowl, whisk together garlic powder, onion powder, ginger, black pepper, soy sauce, honey, and 1 tbsp vegetable oil until combined. Add steak strips and toss to coat.

2. Pour the contents of the bowl into a slow cooker. Add broccoli florets and minced garlic cloves.

3. Cook on low for 6-8 hours, or on high for 3-4 hours, until steak and broccoli are cooked through.

Serve over steamed rice or noodles, and finish with a splinkling of sesame seeds if desired.

Serves 4

PHILLY CHEESESTEAK SANDWICHES

Philly cheesesteak sandwiches are a popular dish made with thinly sliced beef and cheese usually served on a hoagie roll. The sandwich can be made at home by using a slow cooker to cook the beef and then assembling the sandwich with cheese and condiments.

INGREDIENTS

1 LB FLANK STEAK, THINLY SLICED

1/2 CUP BEEF BROTH

1/4 CUP RED WINE VINEGAR

1 TBSP SOY SAUCE

1 TSP DRIED OREGANO

1/4 TSP BLACK PEPPER

1/4 TSP GARLIC POWDER

8 OZ SLICED MUSHROOMS

1 LARGE SLICED ONION

3 TBSP BUTTER

8 OZ SHREDDED CHEESE

6 BAGUETTES OR HOAGIE ROLLS

METHOD

1. In a bowl or a resealable bag, combine the steak, broth, vinegar, soy sauce, oregano, pepper, and garlic powder. Marinate for at least 30 minutes, or up to overnight.

2. In a large skillet over medium-high heat, saute the mushrooms and onion in 2 tbsp of butter until they are soft. Remove the vegetables from the heat and set them aside.

3. In the same skillet, cook the steak until it is browned on both sides.

4. Preheat the slow cooker on Low.

5. Grease the bottom of the slow cooker with 1 tbsp of butter.

6. Layer half of the steak, mushrooms, and onions in the slow cooker. Top with half of the cheese.

7. Repeat the layers once more.

8. Cover and cook for 2-3 hours, or until the steak is cooked through.

9. Serve the sandwich filling on toasted baguettes or hoagie rolls with the remaining cheese melted over them.

Serves 4

TEXAS HASH

his recipe is perfect for a busy day when you want a hearty and satisfying meal with minimal ffort. The beef and vegetables cook in the slow cooker all day, so you come home to a elicious and easy dinner. Serve with some tortilla chips and salsa on the side for a complete eal. Enjoy!

INGREDIENTS

LB GROUND BEEF

ONION, DICED

GREEN BELL PEPPER, DICED

CAN DICED TOMATOES WITH REEN CHILIES

CAN BLACK BEANS, DRAINED ND RINSED

TSP CHILI POWDER

TSP CUMIN

ALT, AND PEPPER, TO TASTE

METHOD

1. In a large skillet over medium heat, cook the beef until browned. Drain any excess fat and remove it from the heat.

2. Add the onion and bell pepper and cook until softened, about 5 minutes. Add the tomatoes, black beans, chili powder, cumin, salt, and pepper to the skillet and stir to combine.

3. Pour the mixture into a slow cooker and cook on low for 6-8 hours.

Serve with shredded cheese and sour cream, if desired.

erves 4

BEEF WITH POTATOES & TURNIPS

Beef Stew with Potatoes, Turnips, and Carrots is a hearty and healthy slow cooker recipe that is perfect for cold winter days. This dish is packed with nutrients, including protein, fiber, vitamins A and C, and potassium. The beef stew also tastes great and is easy to prepare.

INGREDIENTS

1 LB BEEF STEW MEAT

1 LARGE ONION, CHOPPED

3 CLOVES GARLIC, MINCED

2 CARROTS, PEELED AND SLICED INTO THICK ROUNDS

2 SMALL TURNIPS, PEELED AND DICED

1 LB POTATOES, PEELED AND DICED INTO THICK ROUNDS

1 TBSP TOMATO PASTE

1 CUP RED WINE

2 CUPS BEEF BROTH

2 BAY LEAVES

1 SPRIG OF FRESH THYME

2 TBSP BUTTER

SALT, AND PEPPER TO TASTE

METHOD

1. In a large bowl or a zipper-lock bag, combine the beef stew meat, onion, garlic, carrots, turnips, potatoes, tomato paste, red wine, beef broth, bay leaves, thyme, 2 tbsp of butter, salt, and pepper. Mix well, making sure that all of the ingredients are evenly coated.

2. Pour the mixture into a large slow cooker. Cook on low for 8-10 hours, or on high for 4-5 hours, or until the beef and vegetables are tender.

Season with additional salt, and pepper to taste, if desired. Serve hot.

Serves 4

BEEF & BEAN CHILI

his recipe for Beef and Bean Chili is one of our favorites because it is easy-to-make and the low cooker does all the work. The chili can be served with brown rice or tortilla chips, and it makes a hearty meal that will satisfy even the most die-hard chili fan. You can also adapt this recipe to your taste by adding different spices or toppings. Give it a try!

INGREDIENTS

LB GROUND BEEF

CAN KIDNEY BEANS, DRAINED

ND RINSED

CAN BLACK BEANS, DRAINED

ND RINSED

LARGE TOMATO, DICED

GREEN BELL PEPPER, DICED

RED ONION, DICED

CLOVES GARLIC, MINCED

TSP CHILI POWDER

TSP CUMIN

TSP SMOKED PAPRIKA

/2 TSP SALT

/4 TSP BLACK PEPPER

CUPS BEEF BROTH

METHOD

1. In a slow cooker, combine the ground beef, kidney beans, black beans, tomato, bell pepper, red onion, garlic, chili powder, cumin, smoked paprika, salt, pepper, and beef broth.

2. Cover and cook on low for 6 to 8 hours.

Serve hot with rice and toppings of your choice.

TIP If you want a thicker chili, you can use an immersion blender to partially blend the ingredients right in the slow cooker.

erves 4

SWISS STEAK STEW

This easy slow cooker Swiss steak stew is a warm and hearty meal that your whole family wi love. The beef is tender and the sauce is rich and flavorful. Serve this stew with some mashe potatoes or pasta for a complete meal.

INGREDIENTS

1 LB BEEF ROUND STEAK, CUT INTO 1" CUBES

1/2 ONION, DICED

3 CARROTS, PEELED AND SLICED

3 POTATOES, PEELED AND DICED

1 CAN (14.5 OZ) DICED TOMATOES

1/2 CUP BEEF GRAVY

1/2 CUP RED WINE OR BEEF BROTH

1 TBSP WORCESTERSHIRE SAUCE

1 TSP DRIED THYME LEAVES

1/4 TSP PEPPER

METHOD

1. In a large slow cooker, combine the beef cubes, onior carrots, potatoes, tomatoes with juice, gravy mix, red wine c beef broth, Worcestershire sauce, thyme leaves, and peppe

2. Cover and cook on low for 8-9 hours or on high for 4-
hours, stirring occasionally.

Serve over hot cooked pasta, rice, or potatoes.

Serves 4

MISSISSIPPI ROAST BEEF

Mississippi Roast is a delicious, slow cooker recipe that is perfect for busy families. This roast is made with simple ingredients and can be easily customized to fit your family's taste preferences. Best of all, it cooks low and slow in the slow cooker, so you can come home to a delicious, home-cooked meal.

INGREDIENTS

2-3 LB CHUCK STEAK

PACKAGE DRY RANCH DRESSING IX

PACKAGE AU JUS MIX

STICK BUTTER

-10 PEPPERONCINI PEPPERS

METHOD

1. Place the roast in the slow cooker.

2. Combine the dressing mix, Au Jus mix, and butter in a bowl and pour over the roast.

3. Add the pepperoncini peppers to the slow cooker.

4. Cook on low for 8-10 hours or until the roast is falling apart.

Serve with the juices from the slow cooker.

erves 4-6

TACO BEEF
SOUP

This recipe is perfect for a chilly autumn day. The ground beef and vegetables give the soup a hearty texture, while the chili powder and cumin add a spicy flavor. Top with your favorite toppings for a fun and tasty meal.

INGREDIENTS

1 LB GROUND BEEF

1 ONION, CHOPPED

1 GREEN BELL PEPPER, CHOPPED

1 CAN BLACK BEANS, DRAINED
AND RINSED

1 CAN CORN, DRAINED

3 CUPS CHICKEN BROTH

1 TBSP CHILI POWDER

1 TSP CUMIN

1 TSP GARLIC POWDER

SALT, AND PEPPER, TO TASTE

SHREDDED CHEESE, FOR TOPPING

SOUR CREAM, FOR TOPPING

TACO CHIPS, FOR TOPPING

METHOD

1. Add the ground beef, onion, and bell pepper to a slow cooker.

2. In a separate bowl, mix together the black beans, corn, chicken broth, chili powder, cumin, garlic powder, salt, and pepper. Pour the mixture into the slow cooker and mix well.

3. Cook on low for 6-8 hours, or on high for 3-4 hours.

Once cooked, ladle the soup into bowls and top with shredded cheese, sour cream, and taco chips.

Serves 4

CREAMY BEEF STROGANOFF

reamy Beef Stroganoff is a dish that originated in Russia and has become popular throughout ne world. There are many variations of this dish, but the most common ingredients include eef, mushrooms, onions, and sour cream. This dish can be made using a variety of methods, ut the most popular is the slow cooker.

INGREDIENTS

LB BEEF CHUCK STEAK, CUBED

/2 LB MUSHROOMS, SLICED

SMALL ONION, DICED

CLOVES GARLIC, MINCED

TBSP OLIVE OIL

(10.75 OZ) CAN CREAM OF USHROOM SOUP

CUP BEEF BROTH

TBSP WORCESTERSHIRE SAUCE

TSP DRIED THYME LEAVES

/4 TSP BLACK PEPPER

OZ WIDE EGG NOODLES, OOKED AND DRAINED

TBSP SOUR CREAM

TBSP CHOPPED FRESH PARSLEY EAVES

METHOD

1. In a large skillet over medium-high heat, brown the beef chuck steak with the mushrooms, onion, and garlic in olive oil. Drain any excess fat.

2. Add the mushroom soup, beef broth, Worcestershire sauce, thyme, and pepper to the beef mixture. Stir to combine.

3. Place the beef mixture in a 4-quart slow cooker. Cover and cook on low for 6-8 hours, or until the beef is cooked through.

4. About 30 minutes before serving, stir in the cooked noodles and sour cream. Cover and cook on high for another 30 minutes.

Sprinkle with fresh parsley before serving.

erves 4

BEEF WITH WINE & GARLIC

This recipe makes a lot, so feel free to half it if you don't need that much. Also, I like my roas pretty thick, so if you want it more done, adjust the cooking time accordingly. The beauty c the slow cooker is that it's very forgiving! :)

INGREDIENTS

3-4 LB BEEF CHUCK ROAST

1 TSP SALT

1/2 TSP BLACK PEPPER

1 LARGE ONION, SLICED

3 CLOVES GARLIC, MINCED

2 CUPS BEEF BROTH

1/2 CUP RED WINE OR PORT

1 TBSP WORCESTERSHIRE SAUCE

1 TSP DRIED THYME LEAVES

4 CARROTS, PEELED AND ROUGHLY CUBED

4 POTATOES, PEELED AND ROUGHLY CUBED

METHOD

1. Sprinkle the roast with salt and pepper. In a large skille over medium-high heat, brown the roast on all sides. Remov from heat.

2. Add the onion, garlic, beef broth, wine or port, Worcestershir sauce, thyme, carrots, and potatoes to the slow cooker. Ad the roast and any juices that have accumulated in the skillet

3. Cover and cook on low for 8-10 hours, or until the roast i very tender.

4. Remove the roast from the slow cooker and let it rest for 1 minutes before slicing.

Serve with the vegetables from the slow cooker.

Serves 6-8

STUFFED
BELL PEPPERS

One of my favorite things to make in the slow cooker is stuffed bell peppers. I love how easy they are to prep and how delicious they are when they're done. The best part is that you can put just about anything you want in them, so they're perfect for using up leftovers.

INGREDIENTS

BELL PEPPERS, ANY COLOR

LB LEAN GROUND BEEF

SMALL ONION, DICED

GREEN BELL PEPPER, DICED

CAN (15 OZ) BLACK BEANS,
NSED AND DRAINED

CAN (15 OZ) CORN, DRAINED

CAN (14.5 OZ) DICED
OMATOES

TBSP CHILI POWDER

TSP GROUND CUMIN

TSP GARLIC POWDER

2 TSP SALT

4 TSP PEPPER

METHOD

1. Cut off the tops of the bell peppers and remove the seeds. Discard the seeds or save them for another use. Set the peppers aside.

2. In a large skillet over medium-high heat, cook the ground beef until browned. Drain any excess fat and remove it from the heat.

3. Add the onion, green bell pepper, black beans, corn, chili powder, cumin, garlic powder, salt, and pepper to the skillet. Stir until everything is evenly mixed.

4. Spoon the mixture into the bell peppers and place them in a slow cooker.

6. Cook on low for 6-8 hours or on high for 3-4 hours, until the peppers are tender.

Serve with shredded cheese and sour cream, if desired.

Serves 4-6

CLASSIC BEEF STEW

One of the things that makes this beef stew delicious is the use of red wine or beef broth. Thi gives it a richer flavor that makes it irresistible. Additionally, Worcestershire sauce and herb like oregano and thyme add even more flavor to the dish. Finally, carrots and potatoes hel to round out the meal and make it a hearty meal that's ready to serve at the end of the day.

INGREDIENTS

2 LBS BEEF STEW MEAT, CUT INTO 1-INCH CUBES

1/2 TSP SALT

1/4 TSP BLACK PEPPER

1 TBSP VEGETABLE OIL

1 ONION, CHOPPED

3 GARLIC CLOVES, MINCED

1 (14.5 OZ) CAN DICED TOMATOES

1 (6 OZ) CAN TOMATO PASTE

2 TBSP RED WINE OR BEEF BROTH

1 TBSP WORCESTERSHIRE SAUCE

1 TSP DRIED OREGANO

1/2 TSP DRIED THYME

4 CARROTS, CUT INTO 1-INCH SLICES

3 POTATOES, PEELED AND CUT INTO 1-INCH CUBES

METHOD

1. Sprinkle beef with salt, and black pepper. In a large skille or wok, heat oil over high heat. Add beef and onion; stir-fry fo 3 minutes or until beef is browned. Add garlic and tomatoes stir-fry for 2 minutes.

2. Transfer to a slow cooker. Add tomato paste, red wine c beef broth, Worcestershire sauce, oregano, thyme, carrots and potatoes.

3. Cover and cook on low for 6-8 hours or until beef an vegetables are tender.

TIP This dish makes a large amount that's perfect for freezin into batches.

Serves 6-8

PEPPER STEAK

low cooker pepper steak is a delicious and easy-to-make dish. The steak is cooked low and ow in a savory pepper sauce. This dish is perfect for a weeknight meal.

INGREDIENTS

FLANK STEAK **(1 1/2 LBS)**, CUT
TO THIN STRIPS

/2 TSP SALT

/4 TSP BLACK PEPPER

TBSP VEGETABLE OIL

ONION, SLICED

GARLIC CLOVES, MINCED

GREEN BELL PEPPER, SLICED

RED BELL PEPPER, SLICED

(14.5 OZ) CAN DICED

OMATOES

(6 OZ) CAN TOMATO PASTE

TBSP SOY SAUCE

TBSP WORCESTERSHIRE SAUCE

METHOD

1. Sprinkle steak with salt, and black pepper. In a large skillet or wok, heat oil over high heat. Add steak strips and onion; stir-fry for 3 minutes or until steak is browned. Add garlic and bell pepper slices; stir-fry for 2 minutes.

2. Transfer to a 3-quart slow cooker. Add tomatoes, tomato paste, soy sauce, and Worcestershire sauce.

3. cover and cook on low for 6-8 hours or until steak is tender.

Serve over cooked rice.

erves 4-6

MONGOLIAN BEEF STEW

Mongolian beef is a dish that is typically made with flank steak that is thinly sliced and then stir-fried with onions, garlic, and soy sauce. The steak is then coated in a thickened sauce before being served over rice or noodles. While the traditional recipe does call for some time in the kitchen this slow cooker version is quick and easy to prepare leaving you free to get on with your day.

INGREDIENTS

1 1/2 LBS BEEF FLANK STEAK, THINLY SLICED

3 CLOVES GARLIC, MINCED

1/2 TSP GRATED GINGER

1/4 CUP SOY SAUCE

1/4 CUP BEEF BROTH

1/4 CUP BROWN SUGAR, PACKED

3 TBSP VEGETABLE OIL, DIVIDED

1/2 ONION, SLICED

3 GREEN ONIONS, THINLY SLICED

METHOD

1. In a large bowl, combine garlic, ginger, soy sauce, beef broth, brown sugar, and 2 tbsp of the vegetable oil. Add the beef and onion and toss to coat. Cover and refrigerate for at least 2 hours or overnight.

2. In a slow cooker, combine the beef mixture, green onions and the remaining 1 tbsp of oil. Cover and cook on low for 6-8 hours or on high for 3-4 hours.

Serve over cooked rice or noodles.

Serves 4-6

BEEF POT ROAST & VEGETABLES

his pot roast is incredibly delicious and tender. It's perfect for a hearty winter meal. The slow ooker does all the work for you, so it's easy and convenient. Plus, it's a great way to use up ftover vegetables.

INGREDIENTS

3-LB BEEF CHUCK ROAST

TBSP VEGETABLE OIL

LARGE ONION, SLICED

CARROTS, PEELED AND CUT

TO **1**-INCH PIECES

CELERY STALKS, CUT INTO

-INCH PIECES

GARLIC CLOVE, MINCED

CUP BEEF BROTH

TBSP WORCESTERSHIRE SAUCE

TSP DRIED THYME

2 TSP SALT

4 TSP BLACK PEPPER

POTATOES, PEELED AND CUT

TO **1**-INCH PIECES

TBSP CHOPPED FRESH PARSLEY

METHOD

1. In a large skillet over medium-high heat, heat the oil until hot. Add the meat and brown on all sides. Remove from the heat.

2. Add the meat, potatoes, onion, carrots, celery, garlic, broth, Worcestershire sauce, thyme, salt, and pepper to a large slow cooker.

3. Cover and cook on low for 8 to 10 hours or on high for 4 to 5 hours, until the beef is very tender.

4. Remove the roast and vegetables to a serving platter.

5. Skim the fat from the cooking liquid and discard. Serve the sauce over the beef and vegetables. Sprinkle with parsley.

erves 4-6

MAPLE BRAISED BEEF BRISKET

The maple syrup in this recipe gives the beef a delicious sweet and smoky flavor. The briske is cooked low and slow in a slow cooker, which makes it tender and juicy. This recipe i perfect for a busy weeknight because it only takes a few minutes to prepare.

INGREDIENTS

1 BEEF BRISKET **(2-3 LBS)**

1 TBSP OLIVE OIL

1 YELLOW ONION, DICED

2 CLOVES GARLIC, MINCED

1 CUP BEEF STOCK

1/2 CUP MAPLE SYRUP

2 TSP SMOKED PAPRIKA

1 TSP CHILI POWDER

1 TSP CUMIN

1/2 TSP DRIED OREGANO

1/4 TSP SALT

1/4 TSP BLACK PEPPER

METHOD

1. In a slow cooker, combine the beef stock, maple syrup smoked paprika, chili powder, cumin, oregano, salt, an black pepper.

2. Cut the beef brisket into 4 equal portions.

3. Heat the olive oil in a large skillet over medium heat. Coo the onions until softened and add to the slow cooker.

4. Turn up the heat to high and add the beef brisket and coo for 1 minute per side, or until browned.

5. Transfer the beef to the slow cooker. Cover and cook o low for 8-10 hours or on high for 4-5 hours.

6. Remove the beef brisket from the slow cooker and thinl slice.

Serve the sliced beef brisket on a bed of mashed potatoe rice, or quinoa.

Serves 6-8

CHICKEN

Slow cookers are a fantastic way to cook chicken because they are so gentle and slow. The low heat ensures that the chicken cooks evenly and becomes incredibly tender.

Not only does this make the chicken healthier, but it also makes it more flavorful and juicy.

For breasts and thighs, cook it on low for 6-8 hours, or on high for 3-4 hours.

No matter which way you choose to cook your chicken, make sure that it is fully cooked before eating.

CHICKEN CACCIATORE

One of my favorite chicken dishes is chicken cacciatore. I usually make it in the oven, but I also like to make it in the slow cooker. The recipe is really easy-to-make and it's always a hit with my family. Cacciatore means "hunter" in Italian, and the dish is thought to have originated from the Italian countryside. Chicken cacciatore is a simple dish made with chicken, tomatoes, onions, and bell peppers.

INGREDIENTS

1-2 LB CHICKEN THIGHS AND DRUMSTICKS

1/2 TSP SALT

1/4 TSP BLACK PEPPER

1 TBSP OLIVE OIL

1 ONION, CHOPPED

3 GARLIC CLOVES, MINCED

1 RED BELL PEPPER, CHOPPED

1 (14.5 OZ**)** CAN DICED TOMATOES

1 (6 OZ**)** CAN TOMATO PASTE

2 TBSP WHITE WINE OR CHICKEN BROTH

1 TBSP WORCESTERSHIRE SAUCE

1 TSP DRIED OREGANO LEAVES

METHOD

1. Sprinkle chicken with salt, and black pepper. In a large skillet or wok, heat olive oil over high heat. Add chicken and onion; stir-fry for 3 minutes or until chicken is browned. Add garlic and bell pepper; stir-fry for 2 minutes.

2. Transfer to your slow cooker and add tomatoes, tomato paste, white wine or chicken broth, Worcestershire sauce, and oregano leaves.

3. cover and cook on low for 6-8 hours or until chicken is tender.

Serve over cooked pasta, rice, or potatoes.

Serves 4

CHICKEN TERIYAKI

What makes this slow cooker chicken teriyaki delicious is the perfect balance of sweet and savory flavors. The soy sauce and honey create a delicious glaze that coats the chicken breasts, while the garlic and ginger add a wonderful depth of flavor. This dish is perfect for a busy weekday meal, as it is easy to prepare and requires minimal effort if prepared the night before.

INGREDIENTS

4 BONELESS, SKINLESS CHICKEN BREASTS

1/2 CUP SOY SAUCE

1/3 CUP HONEY

1/4 CUP VEGETABLE OIL

3 GARLIC CLOVES, MINCED

1 TSP GROUND GINGER

METHOD

1. In a large resealable bag or container, combine soy sauce, honey, vegetable oil, garlic, and ginger. Add chicken breasts and coat well. Seal bag or container and refrigerate for at least 2 hours, or overnight.

2. When ready to cook place chicken and marinade in the slow cooker.

3. Cover and cook on low for 6-8 hours or until chicken is tender.

Serve over cooked rice.

Serves 4

CHICKEN ROAST
WITH VEGGIES

This recipe is perfect for a busy weeknight! The chicken and vegetables are roasted in the slow cooker all at once, so you don't have to dirty any extra dishes. Put it all in together in the morning and you'll come home to a delicious dinner that's ready to serve. Plus, it's a healthy and hearty meal that the whole family will enjoy!

INGREDIENTS

1 WHOLE CHICKEN

2 TBSP OLIVE OIL

1 LB BABY POTATOES, QUARTERED

1/2 LB CARROTS, PEELED AND SLICED

1/2 CUP CHICKEN BROTH

3 CLOVES GARLIC, MINCED

1 TSP DRIED THYME LEAVES

1/4 TSP BLACK PEPPER

METHOD

1. In a large slow cooker, combine the chicken, potatoes, carrots, chicken broth, garlic, thyme, and pepper.

2. Cover and cook on low for 6-8 hours until the chicken and vegetables are tender.

3. If you prefer your chicken skin crispy, remove it before serving and grill or fry until browned.

Serves 4

GENERAL TSO'S CHICKEN

General Tso's chicken is a popular dish in the United States. It is made with chicken that is breaded and fried and then coated in a sweet and spicy sauce. The dish is often served with rice or noodles. While there are many recipes for General Tso's chicken, most of them involve frying the chicken. However, you can make a healthier version of the dish by using a slow cooker.

INGREDIENTS

1 LB CHICKEN BREAST, CUT INTO SMALL CUBES

2 TBSP VEGETABLE OIL

3 CLOVES GARLIC, MINCED

1/2 ONION, DICED

1/2 CUP CHICKEN BROTH

1/4 CUP SOY SAUCE

1 TBSP RICE VINEGAR

1 TBSP BROWN SUGAR

1 TSP SESAME OIL

1/2 TSP GROUND GINGER

1/4 TSP CHILI POWDER

SESAME SEEDS TO SERVE (OPTIONAL)

METHOD

1. In a large bowl, whisk together chicken broth, soy sauce, rice vinegar, brown sugar, sesame oil, ground ginger, and chili powder.

2. Add chicken cubes to the bowl and coat evenly with the marinade. Let it sit for at least 30 minutes.

3. In a small skillet over medium heat, heat vegetable oil. Add garlic and onion and cook until softened, about 5 minutes.

4. Transfer the chicken and marinade to a slow cooker. Add the cooked garlic and onion and stir well. Set on low and cook for 4-6 hours.

5. Garnish with sesame seeds before serving.

Serves 4

HONEY & SRIRACHA CHICKEN

One of the best things about cooking is that you can make all sorts of different recipes, and each one can be tailored to your own tastes. If you're looking for a delicious and spicy dish, then honey and sriracha chicken is the perfect recipe for you. This slow cooker recipe is easy-to-make and it's sure to impress your friends and family.

INGREDIENTS

1 LB CHICKEN BREAST, CUT INTO CUBES

1/2 ONION, DICED

1 RED BELL PEPPER, DICED

1/2 CUP HONEY

3 TBSP SRIRACHA SAUCE

1 TBSP SOY SAUCE

1/2 TSP GARLIC POWDER

1/4 TSP GROUND GINGER

METHOD

1. In a large bowl, whisk together honey, sriracha sauce, soy sauce, garlic powder, and ground ginger.

2. Add chicken cubes to the bowl and coat evenly with the marinade. Let it sit for at least 30 minutes.

3. Preheat a slow cooker on a low heat setting.

4. Add chicken and vegetables to the slow cooker and cook for 3-4 hours, or until chicken is cooked through.

Serve over rice, quinoa, or noodles, and enjoy!

Serves 4

GREEK STYLE LEMON CHICKEN

If you are looking for a delicious and easy slow cooker recipe, then you should try Greek lemon chicken. This dish is made with chicken breasts, fresh lemon juice, olive oil, garlic, and herbs. You can serve the chicken over rice or pasta, or you can eat it by itself.

INGREDIENTS

1 LB BONELESS, SKINLESS CHICKEN THIGHS

1/2 CUP CHICKEN BROTH

1/4 CUP LEMON JUICE

1/4 CUP OLIVE OIL

2 CLOVES MINCED GARLIC

1 TSP DRIED OREGANO

1/4 TSP SALT

1/4 TSP BLACK PEPPER

METHOD

1. In a large bowl, whisk together chicken broth, lemon juice, olive oil, garlic, oregano, salt, and black pepper.

2. Add the chicken thighs to the bowl with the marinade. Stir to coat and let sit for at least 15 minutes.

3. Pour the chicken and marinade into a slow cooker.

4. Cook on low for 6-8 hours, or on high for 3-4 hours.

5. Serve with roast potatoes or french fries.

Serves 4

CHIPOTLE CHICKEN & WHITE BEAN CHILI

Chipotle chicken and white bean chili is a hearty, flavorful dish that is perfect for a cold winter night. The chili is made with chicken, white beans, chipotle peppers, and tomatoes, and it is slow-cooked to perfection. This chili is sure to please everyone in your family. This recipe makes a lot, so it's great for feeding a crowd. You can also freeze leftovers for another time. Enjoy!

INGREDIENTS

1 LB BONELESS, SKINLESS CHICKEN BREASTS, CUBED

1 CAN (15 OZ) BLACK BEANS, RINSED AND DRAINED

1 CAN (15 OZ) KIDNEY BEANS, RINSED AND DRAINED

1 CAN (14.5 OZ) DICED TOMATOES

1 CAN (6 OZ) TOMATO PASTE

1 CUP CHICKEN BROTH

1 ONION, CHOPPED

3 CLOVES GARLIC, MINCED

2 TSP GROUND CUMIN

1 TSP SMOKED PAPRIKA

1 TSP CHILI POWDER

1/2 TSP SALT

1/4 TSP BLACK PEPPER

1 CHIPOTLE PEPPER IN ADOBO SAUCE

2 TBSP CHOPPED FRESH CILANTRO

Serves 4-6

METHOD

1. In a large bowl, combine the cubed chicken breast, black beans, kidney beans, tomatoes, tomato paste, chicken broth, onion, garlic, cumin, smoked paprika, chili powder, salt, pepper, and chipotle pepper. Pour the mixture into a 4-quart or larger slow cooker.

2. Cover and cook on low for 6-8 hours or on high for 3-4 hours, or until the chicken is cooked through.

3. Stir in the cilantro just before serving.

Serve over rice or tortilla chips.

CHICKEN NOODLE SOUP

There are many different recipes for chicken noodle soup, but all of them have the same goal: to create a delicious, hearty soup that will warm you up and make you feel better. Chicken noodle soup is thought of as the ultimate comfort food, and for good reason: it's delicious, easy-to-make, and good for you. In this article, we'll share some of our favorite slow cooker chicken noodle soup recipes.

INGREDIENTS

1 LB BONELESS, SKINLESS CHICKEN BREASTS

1 LARGE ONION, CHOPPED

4 CARROTS, PEELED AND CHOPPED

3 CELERY STALKS, CHOPPED

2 CLOVES GARLIC, MINCED

1 BAY LEAF

8 CUPS CHICKEN BROTH

1/2 CUP WIDE EGG NOODLES

1 TBSP OLIVE OIL

1/4 CUP CHOPPED FRESH PARSLEY LEAVES (OPTIONAL)

SALT, AND BLACK PEPPER TO TASTE

METHOD

1. Place the chicken breasts in the bottom of a slow cooker. Add the onion, carrots, celery, garlic, bay leaf, chicken broth. Stir to combine.

2. Set the slow cooker to low and cook for 6 to 8 hours, or until the chicken is cooked through and the vegetables are tender.

3. Remove the chicken breasts from the slow cooker and chop them winto bite-sized pieces.

4. Stir the chopped chicken back into the soup and season with salt, and pepper to taste.

Garnish with fresh parsley if desired and serve warm.

Serves 4

HONEY GARLIC CHICKEN

This honey garlic chicken recipe is so good because it is simple to make and the flavors are incredible. You will love the tender chicken thighs cooked in a savory sauce made with honey, soy sauce, ketchup, and garlic. This is one meal you'll want to make again and again!

INGREDIENTS

1 1/2 LBS CHICKEN DRUMSTICKS

1 LARGE ONION, SLICED

3 CLOVES GARLIC, MINCED

1 CUP HONEY

1/4 CUP SOY SAUCE

2 TBSP KETCHUP

1 TSP DRIED OREGANO

1/2 TSP SMOKED PAPRIKA

1/4 TSP CAYENNE PEPPER

SALT, AND BLACK PEPPER TO TASTE

METHOD

1. Season the chicken drumsticks with salt, pepper, and oregano. In a large skillet over medium-high heat, brown the chicken on all sides until golden brown. Remove from heat and set aside.

2. In the same skillet, saute the onions until they are softened. Add the garlic and cook for an additional minute. Stir in the honey, soy sauce, ketchup, oregano, smoked paprika, cayenne pepper, and chicken.

3. Pour the contents of the skillet into a slow cooker and cook on low for 6-8 hours or on high for 3-4 hours.

Serve over rice or noodles.

Serves 4

CHICKEN KORMA

Slow cooker Chicken Korma is a wonderfully fragrant dish that is perfect for busy weeknights. The chicken is slow-cooked in a creamy coconut milk sauce, seasoned with Indian spices such as cumin, turmeric, and garam masala. This dish is best served with steamed white rice and a garnish of cilantro leaves. Enjoy!

INGREDIENTS

4 CHICKEN BREASTS, CUBED

1 ONION, CHOPPED

1 GARLIC CLOVE, CRUSHED

2 TSP GRATED GINGER

2 TBSP OIL

1 TSP GROUND CUMIN

1 TSP TURMERIC

2 TSP GARAM MASALA

400ML/14FL OZ CAN COCONUT MILK

1 LIME JUICED

SALT, AND BLACK PEPPER

CILANTRO LEAVES, TO GARNISH

METHOD

1. In a bowl, combine the onion, garlic, ginger, and oil.

2. Add the chicken and spices and mix well.

3. Spread the mixture in the slow cooker.

4. Pour in the coconut milk and lime juice and season with salt, and pepper.

5. Cook on low for 6-8 hours or on high for 3-4 hours until the chicken is cooked through.

6. Serve with white rice and garnish with cilantro leaves.

Serves 4

CREAMY MEXICAN CHICKEN

This dish is perfect for a busy weeknight meal. The slow cooker does all the work for you and it's packed with flavor. You can also customize this recipe to your liking by adding different types of beans or vegetables. Give it a try!

INGREDIENTS

1 1/2 LBS CHICKEN BREAST, SLICED

1 ONION, DICED

1 RED BELL PEPPER, DICED

2 CLOVES GARLIC, MINCED

1 TSP CHILI POWDER

1 TSP CUMIN

1/2 TSP SALT

1/4 TSP BLACK PEPPER

14.5 OZ CAN DICED TOMATOES

15 OZ CAN BLACK BEANS, RINSED AND DRAINED

4 OZ CAN DICED GREEN CHILIES, UNDRAINED

3/4 CUP CHICKEN BROTH

1/2 CUP HEAVY CREAM

1 TBSP FRESH LIME JUICE

METHOD

1. Add chicken, onion, bell pepper, garlic, chili powder, cumin, salt, pepper, tomatoes with juice, black beans, green chilies, chicken broth, and cream to a large slow cooker and stir well.

2. Cover and cook on low heat for 6-8 hours or on high heat for 3-4 hours.

3. Stir in lime juice just before serving.

Serves 4

BUTTER CHICKEN

If you need an easy dish for those busy weekday nights, call on my slow cooker Butter Chicken because you'll be glad that you did. The spices are savory and the sauce is rich with tomato essence, making it a dish that you'll come back to time and time again. Plus, it's perfect for serving a large crowd. So go ahead—put this recipe to the test! You won't regret it.

INGREDIENTS

1 LB BONELESS, SKINLESS CHICKEN THIGHS

1 ONION, DICED

1 RED BELL PEPPER, DICED

1 TBSP GARLIC POWDER

1 TSP GARAM MASALA

1 TSP GROUND CORIANDER

1 TSP GROUND CUMIN

1/2 TSP TURMERIC

1/2 TSP SALT

1/4 TSP BLACK PEPPER

2 TBSP BUTTER

1 (14.5 OZ) CAN DICED TOMATOES

3/4 CUP CHICKEN BROTH

1 TBSP HONEY

3 TBSP TOMATO PASTE

1 TBSP CORNSTARCH DISSOLVED IN 1 TBSP WATER

METHOD

1. In a small bowl, whisk together garlic powder, garam masala, coriander, cumin, turmeric, salt, and black pepper.

2. Rub the spice mixture all over the chicken thighs.

3. In a large skillet over medium heat, melt butter. Add onion and bell pepper and cook until soft, about 5 minutes.

4. Transfer the onion and bell pepper to a 6-quart slow cooker. Add chicken, tomatoes with juice, chicken broth, honey, and tomato paste.

5. Cover and cook on low for 6 to 8 hours or on high for 3 to 4 hours.

6. In a small bowl, whisk together cornstarch and water. Stir into the slow cooker and cook on high for 15 minutes, or until thickened.

Serve over cooked rice or couscous. Enjoy!

Serves 4

CHICKEN & CREAMY MUSHROOM SAUCE

This recipe is perfect for those who want a hearty and creamy dish, without having to spend hours in the kitchen. Simply pop all of the ingredients into your slow cooker, and let it do its thing while you go about your day. When you get home you'll have a delicious and satisfying meal waiting for you. Enjoy!

INGREDIENTS

1 LB BONELESS, SKINLESS CHICKEN BREASTS, CUBED

1 CAN CREAM OF MUSHROOM SOUP

1/4 CUP SOUR CREAM

1 TSP DRIED THYME LEAVES

3/4 TSP SALT

1/4 TSP BLACK PEPPER

8 OZ SLICED MUSHROOMS

1 TBSP BUTTER

2 TBSP ALL-PURPOSE FLOUR

1/2 CUPS CHICKEN BROTH

1/4 CUP DRY WHITE WINE OR VERMOUTH

1 TBSP WORCESTERSHIRE SAUCE

METHOD

1. In a slow cooker, combine the chicken, soup, milk, sour cream, thyme, salt, and pepper. Stir in the mushrooms.

2. In a small saucepan, melt the butter over medium heat. Stir in the flour and continue to stir until the mixture is smooth. Gradually whisk in the broth, wine or vermouth, and Worcestershire sauce. Bring to a boil, stirring constantly. Pour over the chicken mixture in the slow cooker.

3. Cover and cook on a Low-heat setting for 6 to 8 hours or a High-heat setting for 3 to 4 hours.

4. Serve the chicken mixture over hot cooked pasta, rice, or potatoes.

Serves 4

PORK

Slow cooker pork is a great way to have a juicy and tender piece of meat. With little effort, the pork can be cooked to perfection in the slow cooker.

The long cooking time will break down the tough fibers in the meat, making it more tender and you'll come home to a delicious and filling meal.

One of the most rewarding cuts of meat you can cook in a slow cooker is pork shoulder. It is an inexpensive, easy to prepare cut of meat that really shines when cooked low and slow.

SZECHUAN PORK WITH BROCCOLI

If you're looking for a delicious and easy slow cooker recipe, look no further than Szechuan pork with broccoli. This dish is packed with flavor and takes just minutes to prepare, the pork is cooked in a savory Asian sauce and served with tender broccoli florets. It's perfect for busy weeknight meal or a special occasion so why not give it a try?

INGREDIENTS

1 LB BONELESS PORK LOIN, TRIMMED AND CUT INTO **1**-INCH PIECES

3 CLOVES GARLIC, MINCED

1 TSP GRATED GINGERROOT

1/2 TSP RED PEPPER FLAKES

1/4 CUP SOY SAUCE

1/4 CUP CHICKEN BROTH

3 TBSP DRY SHERRY OR RICE VINEGAR

3 TBSP BROWN SUGAR, PACKED

1 TBSP CORNSTARCH

4 CUPS BROCCOLI FLORETS

METHOD

1. Combine the pork, garlic, ginger root, red pepper flakes, soy sauce, chicken broth, sherry or rice vinegar, brown sugar and cornstarch in your slow cooker.

2. Stir well and add the broccoli florets.

3. Cover and cook on a low-heat setting for 6 to 7 hours or high-heat setting for 3 to 3 1/2 hours.

Serve over cooked rice.

Serves 4

SLOW-COOKED PORK SHOULDER

ork shoulder is a tough, flavorful cut that is best cooked slowly in moist heat. There are many ifferent ways to cook a pork roast, but one of the most popular methods is to slow cook it in slow cooker. A pork roast cooked in a slow cooker is tender, juicy, and full of flavor.

INGREDIENTS

LB PORK SHOULDER

TSP SALT

/4 TSP BLACK PEPPER

TBSP OLIVE OIL

ONION, CHOPPED

GARLIC CLOVES, MINCED

(14.5 OZ) CAN DICED

OMATOES

(6 OZ) CAN TOMATO PASTE

TBSP WHITE WINE OR CHICKEN

ROTH

TBSP WORCESTERSHIRE SAUCE

TSP DRIED OREGANO LEAVES

METHOD

1. Sprinkle pork roast with salt, and black pepper. In a large skillet or wok, heat olive oil over high heat. Add pork and onion; stir-fry for 3 minutes or until pork is browned. Add garlic and tomatoes; stir-fry for 2 minutes.

2. Transfer to your slow cooker. Add tomato paste, white wine or chicken broth, Worcestershire sauce, and oregano leaves.

3. Cover and cook on low for 6-8 hours or until pork is tender.

Serve over cooked pasta, rice, or potatoes.

erves 4-6

PULLED PORK
& BBQ SAUCE

One of the best things about a slow cooker is that you can make a dish like pulled pork that i both delicious and easy to make. The pork roast will cook in the slow cooker until it is tende and falls apart, then you can shred it with a fork and mix it with the barbecue sauce.

INGREDIENTS

2-3 LBS PORK SHOULDER

1 CUP APPLE JUICE OR CIDER

FOR THE BARBECUE SAUCE:

1 TSP GARLIC POWDER

1 TSP ONION POWDER

1 TSP PAPRIKA

1 TSP SALT

1/2 TSP BLACK PEPPER

1/2 CUP APPLE CIDER VINEGAR

1/4 CUP KETCHUP

3 TBSP BROWN SUGAR, PACKED

2 TSP DRY MUSTARD

1 TSP WORCESTERSHIRE SAUCE

1/4 TSP CAYENNE PEPPER

METHOD

1. Chop the pork into 5-6 chunks and fry in a large pan unt browned.

2. Add pork and apple juice or cider to the slow cooker.

3. Cover and cook on low for 8-10 hours, or on high for 4- hours, until the pork is cooked through and falls apart.

4. Combine all of the ingredients for the barbecue sauce an stir well.

5. Remove the pork from the slow cooker and discard th cooking liquid.

6. Shred the pork with two forks and return it to the slow cooke with the barbecue sauce.

7. Cover and cook on low for another 30-60 minutes, until th pork is heated through.

Serve on buns with your favorite toppings.

Serves 6-8

SAUSAGE & PEPPERS

low cooker sausage and peppers is one of the easiest and most delicious dishes you will ver make in your slow cooker! This dish is perfect for a busy night when you don't have a lot f time to cook. The sausage and peppers will cook all day in the slow cooker and by dinner me, you will have a delicious, hearty meal that the whole family will love!

INGREDIENTS

LB SAUSAGES

GREEN BELL PEPPER, DICED

RED BELL PEPPER, DICED

YELLOW ONION, DICED

(14 OZ) CAN DICED TOMATOES

(6 OZ) CAN TOMATO PASTE

CLOVES GARLIC, MINCED

TSP DRIED BASIL LEAVES

2 TSP SALT

4 TSP BLACK PEPPER

CUPS PASTA

RATED PARMESAN CHEESE TO

ERVE

METHOD

1. In a large skillet over medium heat, cook sausage, bell peppers, and onion until sausage is browned; drain.

2. In a large slow cooker, mix tomatoes, tomato paste, garlic, basil, salt, and pepper. Add sausage mixture and stir well.

3. Cover and cook on a low-heat setting for 6 to 8 hours or a high-heat setting for 3 to 4 hours.

4. Around 30 minutes before the end of cooking add the pasta and stir well.

If desired, sprinkle with Parmesan cheese before serving.

MUSTARD RUBBED PORK LOIN

One of the best things about a slow cooker is that you can put in meat and vegetable and have a complete meal with very little effort. This mustard rubbed pork loin is a perfect example. The pork is rubbed with a mixture of Dijon mustard, garlic, and herbs, then cooked in the slow cooker with root vegetables. The result is a tender, flavorful pork loin that's perfect for a winter meal.

INGREDIENTS

1 PORK LOIN

2 TBSP OLIVE OIL

2 TBSP DIJON MUSTARD

1 TBSP SMOKED PAPRIKA

1 TBSP BROWN SUGAR

1 TSP GARLIC POWDER

1 TSP ONION POWDER

1 TSP SALT

1/2 TSP BLACK PEPPER

METHOD

1. In a bowl, whisk together the olive oil, Dijon mustard smoked paprika, brown sugar, garlic powder, onion powder salt, and black pepper.

2. Rub the mixture all over the pork loin.

3. Place the pork in a slow cooker and cook on low for 6- hours or high for 3-4 hours.

4. When the pork is cooked through, slice it into thin strips.

Serve with rice or mashed potatoes.

Serves 4

CHEESY BACON POTATOES

heesy Bacon Potatoes is one of the best slow cooker recipes that you can make. This dish simple to prepare, and it is loaded with flavor. The cheese and bacon add a delicious flavor the potatoes.

INGREDIENTS

POTATOES, PEELED AND SLICED

2 LB BACON, CHOPPED

ONION, DICED

CUPS SHREDDED CHEDDAR
HEESE

CUP MILK

TBSP GARLIC POWDER

TBSP ONION POWDER

TSP SALT

2 TSP BLACK PEPPER

METHOD

1. Add potatoes, bacon, onion, cheese, milk, garlic powder, onion powder, salt, and pepper to the slow cooker. Mix well.

2. Cook on low for 6 to 8 hours or on high for 3 to 4 hours, until potatoes are tender and cheese is melted and serve.

erves 4

TERIYAKI PORK LOIN

This teriyaki pork recipe is so good because it is made with a delicious and flavorful teriyaki sauce. The pork is tender and juicy, and the teriyaki sauce gives it a perfect balance of sweet and savory flavors. It's the perfect blend of flavors for a delicious and easy-to-make dish!

INGREDIENTS

1 PORK LOIN

1 CUP SOY SAUCE

1 CUP CHICKEN BROTH

3/4 CUP BROWN SUGAR

1/4 CUP APPLE CIDER VINEGAR

2 TBSP SESAME OIL

3 CLOVES GARLIC, MINCED

1 TSP GROUND GINGER

1/4 TSP BLACK PEPPER

METHOD

1. Cut the pork loin into 1-inch cubes.

2. In a large bowl, whisk together the soy sauce, chicken broth, brown sugar, apple cider vinegar, sesame oil, garlic, ginger, and black pepper.

3. Place the pork cubes into the slow cooker and pour the sauce over top. Cook on low for 6-8 hours or on high for 3-4 hours.

Serve over rice and enjoy!

Serves 4

BARBECUE RIBS

his recipe is perfect for a lazy weekend day. The ribs cook slowly in the slow cooker and ome out tender and juicy. The sauce is a perfect mix of spicy and sweet and goes great with arbecue sauce. So next time you're looking for something easy-to-make, give these slow ooker barbecue ribs a try!

INGREDIENTS

RACK OF PORK RIBS

CUP OF KETCHUP

'2 CUP OF WHITE VINEGAR

'4 CUP OF BROWN SUGAR

TBSP OF PAPRIKA

TBSP OF CHILI POWDER

TSP OF GARLIC POWDER

'2 TSP OF ONION POWDER

'4 TSP OF CAYENNE PEPPER

METHOD

1. In a small bowl, whisk together the ketchup, vinegar, brown sugar, paprika, chili powder, garlic powder, onion powder, and cayenne pepper. Set aside.

2. Cut the rack of ribs into 3 or 4 equal portions. Season the ribs all over with salt, and black pepper. Place the ribs in the slow cooker. Pour the ketchup mixture over the ribs.

3. Cook on low for 6-8 hours, or until the ribs are very tender.

4. Remove the ribs from the slow cooker and discard any excess sauce.

Serve hot with your favorite barbecue sauce. Enjoy!

erves 4

MEAT FREE

Choosing meat free options helps to conserve precious resources. Meatless meals can be just as delicious and satisfying as those with meat, and they're often healthier too.

Slow cookers are a great way to cook hearty vegetarian meals. The low heat cooks the food slowly and evenly, which results in tender, flavorful dishes. Plus, there's no need to babysit a pot on the stove – just put everything in the slow cooker and let it do its thing. This hands-off cooking method is perfect for busy vegetarians who want a home-cooked meal without having to spend hours in the kitchen.

MEAT FREE
MEXICAN MANICOTTI

Mexican manicotti is a dish that is made up of pasta shells that are filled with a cheese mixture. The mixture is then topped with a sauce and cheese, and it is baked in the oven. Mexican manicotti can be made in a slow cooker, and it is a great dish to make for a potluck or party.

INGREDIENTS

1 (15 OZ) CAN BLACK BEANS, RINSED AND DRAINED

10 OZ RICOTTA CHEESE

1/2 CUP CHOPPED ONION

1/2 CUP CHOPPED RED BELL PEPPER

1/4 CUP CHOPPED FRESH PARSLEY

3 GARLIC CLOVES, MINCED

1 TSP GROUND CUMIN

1/4 TSP SALT

1/4 TSP BLACK PEPPER

8 MANICOTTI SHELLS

1 1/2 CUPS SHREDDED MONTEREY JACK CHEESE

METHOD

1. In a medium bowl, combine black beans, ricotta cheese, onion, bell pepper, parsley, garlic, cumin, salt, and black pepper.

2. Stuff the mixture into the manicotti shells. Arrange shells in the slow cooker.

3. Pour tomato sauce over shells. Sprinkle with cheese.

4. Bake for 2-4 hours or until pasta is cooked and cheese is melted and bubbly.

Serves 4

CHICKPEA CURRY

Chickpea curry is a delicious, nutritious dish that can be made in a slow cooker. Chickpeas are a great source of protein and fiber, and the spices used in curry dishes can help to improve your digestion. This particular recipe is simple to make and only requires a few ingredients. The resulting dish is flavorful and filling, perfect for a winter meal.

INGREDIENTS

1 ONION, DICED

1 RED PEPPER, DICED

1 TBSP OLIVE OIL

2 CLOVES GARLIC, MINCED

1 TSP GRATED GINGER

2 TSP GROUND CUMIN

1 TSP SMOKED PAPRIKA

1 TSP TURMERIC

400G CAN CHICKPEAS, DRAINED AND RINSED

400ML CAN COCONUT MILK

200G BABY SPINACH LEAVES

1 LIME JUICED

SEA SALT AND BLACK PEPPER TO TASTE

METHOD

1. In a large frying pan over medium heat, saute onions and red pepper in olive oil until softened.

2. Add garlic, ginger, cumin, smoked paprika, turmeric, and chickpeas. Cook for 2-3 minutes until fragrant.

3. Transfer to a slow cooker. Add coconut milk and spinach leaves.

4. Cook for 2-3 hours on low heat or until heated through. Season with lime juice, salt, and pepper to taste.

Serve with steamed rice or naan bread.

Serves 4

ALOO GOBI

Aloo gobi is a dish made from potatoes and cauliflower. It is a popular dish in Indian cuisine. The ingredients are simple, but the flavor is complex. This dish can be made in a slow cooker, making it easy to prepare. If you're looking for an easy and delicious slow cooker dish, give this Aloo Gobi recipe a try! You won't be disappointed.

INGREDIENTS

1 LB CAULIFLOWER FLORETS

1 LARGE POTATO, PEELED AND DICED

1 TBSP VEGETABLE OIL

1 TSP CUMIN SEEDS

1 TSP GROUND GINGER

1/2 TSP GROUND TURMERIC

1/4 TSP CAYENNE PEPPER

1/2 CUP WATER

1/2 CUP PLAIN YOGURT

3 TBSP CHOPPED FRESH CILANTRO LEAVES

SALT TO TASTE

METHOD

1. In a large bowl, combine the cauliflower, potato, oil, cumin seeds, ginger, turmeric, cayenne pepper, and water.

2. Stir well and pour into the slow cooker.

3. Cover and cook on low for 6 to 8 hours or on high for 3 to 4 hours, until the vegetables are tender.

Stir in the yogurt, cilantro leaves, and salt to taste.

Tip This dish is perfect with a side of naan bread!

Serves 4

QUINOA PILAF

Quinoa is a popular superfood that is often used in salads and stir-frys. However, did you know that you can also cook quinoa in a slow cooker? This quinoa pilaf recipe is a great way to make a healthy and filling side dish. The best part is that it only takes about 10 minutes to prepare.

INGREDIENTS

1 CUP QUINOA, RINSED

1 CUP VEGETABLE BROTH

1 CAN CHICKPEAS, DRAINED AND RINSED

1/2 RED ONION, DICED

1 RED BELL PEPPER, DICED

1/4 CUP CILANTRO, CHOPPED

2 CLOVES GARLIC, MINCED

1 TSP GROUND CUMIN

1/4 TSP SALT

1/4 TSP BLACK PEPPER

METHOD

1. In a large bowl, combine quinoa, vegetable broth, chickpeas, red onion, red bell pepper, cilantro, garlic, cumin, salt, and black pepper.

2. Mix well and add the mixture to a slow cooker.

3. Cook on low for 6-8 hours, or until quinoa is cooked through.

Serves 4

LENTIL DAL

Slow cooker lentil dal is a healthy, hearty, vegan meal that is perfect for a winter day. The spices and herbs give this dish a wonderful flavor, and the lentils are cooked until tender. It is a vegan dish that is high in protein and fiber. This dal is sure to please everyone at your table!

INGREDIENTS

1 CUP LENTILS, RINSED

2 CUPS VEGETABLE BROTH

1 ONION, CHOPPED

3 CLOVES GARLIC, MINCED

1 TSP GROUND CUMIN

1 TSP GROUND CORIANDER

1/2 TSP GROUND GINGER

PINCH OF CAYENNE PEPPER

1 CUP RED LENTILS, RINSED

4 CUPS VEGETABLE BROTH

1 LARGE ONION, CHOPPED

6 CLOVES GARLIC, MINCED

2 TSP GROUND CUMIN

2 TSP GROUND CORIANDER

1 TSP TURMERIC

1/2 TSP GROUND GINGER

PINCH OF CAYENNE PEPPER

SALT AND FRESHLY GROUND

BLACK PEPPER TO TASTE

FRESH CILANTRO FOR GARNISH

METHOD

1. In a large saucepan, combine the lentils, broth, onion, garlic, cumin, coriander, ginger, and cayenne pepper. Bring to a boil over medium-high heat. Lower the heat to maintain a simmer and cook until the lentils are tender - about 30 minutes.

2. Remove from the heat and stir in the red lentils.

3. In a large slow cooker, combine the lentil mixture, broth, onion, garlic, cumin, coriander, turmeric, ginger, and cayenne pepper. Season with salt, and black pepper to taste. Cook on low until the lentils are tender, about 6 hours.

4. To serve, ladle the dal into bowls and garnish with cilantro. Serve hot.

Serves 4

CHILI SIN CARNE

Chili sin carne, also known as chili without meat, is a popular vegan dish made from chili peppers, tomatoes, and spices. While there are many variations of this dish, most recipes call for a slow cooker to cook the ingredients low and slow. Chili sin carne is perfect for a winter meal, and can easily be made in bulk to serve a large crowd.

INGREDIENTS

1 LARGE ONION, DICED

3 CLOVES GARLIC, MINCED

1 BELL PEPPER, DICED

1 JALAPENO PEPPER, DICED

2 TBSP OLIVE OIL

2 TBSP CHILI POWDER

1 TSP CUMIN

1 TSP SMOKED PAPRIKA

1 TSP OREGANO

1/2 TSP SALT

1/4 TSP BLACK PEPPER

2 CANS DICED TOMATOES

1 CAN BLACK BEANS, RINSED

1 CAN KIDNEY BEANS, RINSED

1 CAN PINTO BEANS, RINSED

1 CAN CRUSHED TOMATOES

1/2 CUP TOMATO SAUCE

1/2 CUP WATER

1/4 CUP CHOPPED FRESH CILANTRO

METHOD

1. In a large skillet over medium heat, saute onions, garlic, bell pepper, and jalapeno pepper in olive oil until softened.

2. Add chili powder, cumin, smoked paprika, oregano, salt, and black pepper, and cook for 1 minute longer.

3. Transfer to a slow cooker and add tomatoes, black beans, kidney beans, pinto beans, tomato sauce, and water.

4. Cover and cook on low for 6-8 hours or on high for 3-4 hours. Just before serving, stir in fresh cilantro.

Serve with shredded cheese, sour cream, and chopped green onions, if desired.

Serves 4-6

MUSHROOM STROGANOFF

Mushroom stroganoff is a Russian dish that has been around for centuries. The original dish was made with beef, but it can also be made with pork, lamb, or chicken. The modern version of the dish usually contains mushrooms, onions, sour cream, and Dijon mustard. It can be served over pasta, rice, or potatoes. Mushroom stroganoff is a hearty and comforting dish that is perfect for cold winter nights.

INGREDIENTS

1 LB SLICED MUSHROOMS

1/2 CUP CHOPPED ONION

1/4 CUP FLOUR

1 1/2 CUPS VEGETABLE BROTH

1 TBSP WORCESTERSHIRE SAUCE

1 TBSP PAPRIKA

10 OZ SOURED CREAM

1 TSP SALT

1/4 TSP BLACK PEPPER

1 BAY LEAF

3 TBSP BUTTER

8 OZ FRESH SLICED WIDE EGG

NOODLES

METHOD

1. In a large skillet, cook mushrooms, onion, paprika, and flour over medium heat until the vegetables are tender.

2. Transfer to a slow cooker. Add the beef broth, Worcestershire sauce, salt, black pepper, and bay leaf.

3. Cover and cook on low for 6-8 hours.

4. About 30 minutes before serving add the soured cream to the slow cooker and stir through, Melt the butter in a large saucepan. Add cooked noodles and stir until well coated.

5. Serve the stroganoff over the noodles.

Serves 4

PUMPKIN & GINGER COCONUT CURRY

Enjoy this easy and delicious slow cooker Pumpkin & Ginger Coconut Curry! This dish is perfect for a chilly fall evening. The coconut milk gives the curry a creamy and decadent texture, while the pumpkin adds a touch of sweetness and earthiness. You can also adjust the spiciness to your liking by adding more or less Thai red curry paste. Enjoy!

INGREDIENTS

1 CAN (15 OZ) PUMPKIN PUREE

1 SMALL PUMPKIN OR BUTTERNUT SQUASH CUBED

1 CAN (13.5 OZ) COCONUT MILK

2 TBSP THAI RED CURRY PASTE

1 TBSP HONEY

1 TSP GROUND GINGER

1/2 TSP GROUND CORIANDER

1/4 TSP GROUND CUMIN

KOSHER SALT AND FRESHLY GROUND BLACK PEPPER, TO TASTE

3 CUPS COOKED JASMINE RICE

1/2 CUP CHOPPED FRESH CILANTRO LEAVES

METHOD

1. In a slow cooker, combine pumpkin puree, cubed pumpkin or butternut squash coconut milk, Thai red curry paste, honey, ground ginger, coriander, and cumin; season with salt, and pepper, to taste.

2. Cover and cook on low heat for 6-8 hours or until heated through.

Serve over Jasmine rice, garnished with cilantro leaves.

Serves 4

Printed in Great Britain
by Amazon

37479238R00066